# as the

# moon

# has

# breath

**doris ferleger**

MAIN STREET RAG PUBLISHING COMPANY
CHARLOTTE, NORTH CAROLINA

Acknowledgments: I would like to thank the editors of the following literary journals in which these poems first appeared, sometimes in different versions:

*Alembic*: "Jump"
*Baltimore Review*: "Instead of Angels"
*The Cortland Review*: "Farthest from the Moon,"
    "Morning Was Snow"
*L.A. Review*: "Five Full Moons"
*Madison Review*: "Invincible"
*The New Guard Literary Review*: "Now the Smoke Bushes"
*New Letters*: "In the Bardo of Dying," "Now That You Are Spirit,"
    "As the Moon Has Breath" (formerly titled "Ordinary")
*Poet Lore*: "What I Mean by Beauty"
*Quiddity*: "Call and Response"
*Schuylkill Valley Journal*: "Embrace," "How Do You Love Your
    Life?"
*South Dakota Review*: "For Example"
*Talking River*: "Lost Is Not a Place"
*When You Become Snow* (Finishing Line Press): "Shiva: God of Mercy,
    God of Destruction," "Saying Your Name," "On His Palm,"
    "When You Become Snow"

Library of Congress Control Number: 2013935417

ISBN: 978-1-59948-421-1

Produced in the United States of America

Main Street Rag
PO Box 690100
Charlotte, NC 28227
**www.MainStreetRag.com**

*In loving and blessed memory
and with deepest gratitude for:*

*My beloved husband, Steven Carl Halbert*
*My beloved Momma, Miriam Ferleger*
*My beloved Poppa, Albert (Abram) Ferleger*

# CONTENTS

## PART III

## INVOCATION

*The trees*
*and the birds in the trees had been singing so long together*
*that no one on the ground would have thought to distinguish*
*the bird from the tree.* —David Simpson

To words, and to the limits
of words that make us trill and coo,
rasp and moan, plead and sigh

like tree-birds that fly
their heavy trunks and blue beaks
over the impossible garden—

to the blind poet who reminds me
the tree and the bird are the same
breathing song, and not the same—

that it all depends on whether we hear
with our eyes, or the millions
of eyes and hands and ears

inside the body—that we all must,
in the course of a lifetime,
listen with roots and eyes,

must sing everything we know—
though we will not be saved,
we will be sung to.

# PART I

## COUNT STARS

Because strength is your sister
whom you have called selfishness,

because grief is your brother who has lived
with you too long, because too much

fear leads to loneliness,
because you are lonely,

because beauty spills like milk
from the moon and there is no one

beside you to see the stars form
dippers that tip

toward your mouth
because your mouth wants so much.

## PRZEŚCIERADŁO (PSHE•SHCHE•RA•DLWO):
## THE POLISH WORD FOR SHEET


was the first thing you loved to play with in your mouth,
put your lips together for, then quickly part them just in time
to curl convex tongue against pallet to form the *psh-psh-pshing*
sound new mothers instinctively make,

though now it's official, written up in baby books—
*Protocol sound prevents shaken-baby syndrome.* Seriously—
rock the child in his little rocky chair with the seat belt
fastened and repeat *psh-psh-psh* rapidly—

mouth and tongue fully engaged in a loud whisper,
this is better than to sing, better than to make one shushing
sound after another—as in *sh, sh, sh*, which only serves
to make the baby want to holler even louder. *Pshe•shche•ra•dlwo*—

you have to go right from the *sh-sh* to the *ch* in the same syllable,
and you are five years old and no one at school makes these sounds
and your teacher has no idea that you make these sounds
under your breath at school and aloud at home,

without ever stopping to think how the tongue
is required to switch in a split second from *pshing*
to striking the ridge of the palate to make the *ch* sound,
and how to let go right away in order to taste

the two sounds in tandem that belong to that
outrageously wonderful word, *pshe•shche•ra•dlwo*
that belongs to you—your family secret—you think
about these things over milk and cookies that you eat

alone at a big low table. You don't know why
you are alone, except for the sounds, the *sh* and *ch* that
sit so close to each other—inseparable, in your row house
overlooking the trolleys. Once you found two *ch* sounds

in the same word, a very short word, *church*, that belonged
to the fair-skinned girls on the street who wore short white
gloves and gingham dresses on Sundays while you lay beneath
complex syllables of *pshe•shche•ra•dlwo*, tongue twister in Polish—

Mother tongue that saved your father's life—
Mother tongue that sold out a Jew for a stick of butter—
Mother tongue your grandmother scrubbed from the mouths
of her children—only the *Oys* of *Yiddish* allowed to huddle

in each doomed hiding place. Mother tongue
your own mother spoke most carefree in your childhood—
how she coupled the *psh-psh-pshing* sound with the *ch* sound
and covered the two of you so close together.

## FARTHEST FROM THE MOON

In the parking lot at dusk only the children can see the moon
is near, much nearer than, say, Jordan, Syria, Egypt or Israel.
Under the close moon, in a father's arms, a little girl reaches up:

*Moon, moon!* How the light pulls her like a great wave.
*Look daddy, see's tying her sooz,* the son points from his stroller
as he twirls his long curls the color of jonquils and sun.

The boy says the sentence three times, but his *sh* sounds
stay stuck under the roof of his mouth. The father says,
*Yesss, umm humm,* in that high falsetto voice used

when we have no clue of what a child is saying.
But the boy will stop only if the father repeats the phrase
in a way that shows he gets how hard the boy is working

for his words. Finally, the father sees and though the boy
is silent now and looks quite satisfied, the father feels a need
to translate his son to me, *Yes, the lady is tying her shoes!*

As if I hadn't understood either, as if my understanding
his son might help me with my worries about my own son
who sleeps in a hut in the Sinai where sound comes

from my son only when I phone him and he complains
of stomach pain, the only call that's gone through in weeks
and I waste words, pronounce them as if he were a small child,

words like: hospital. *How far?* He answers: *Impossible to tell
you've stepped from the land of Israel into the land of Egypt
or back again except for the border patrol, passport police,*

*police patting down bodies, and the different kinds of cats.*
*Did you know the Dead Sea is the lowest place on earth?*
Does that mean it's farthest from the moon?

## MORNING WAS SNOW

*What I did?*
*    Liberation day?*

*         I tell you*
*              like it is happening now.*

*                   I stand under a tree. What kind,*
*                        you want*

*I should know? My mouth,*
*    I can't believe*

*         breathes*
*              with no one*

*                   measuring the amount of air*
*                        I steal. I don't pray*

*                             to remember. I don't pray*
*                                  not to remember*

*that night, the walls*
*    not just wailing.*

*         You think this is wailing        here*
*              with these Chassids shukkling,*

*                   rocking, pulling*
*                        beards. Mouths full*

*                        of prayers.*
*                             They believe.    Still.*

*Good for them.*
         *They're doing what they survived to do. Wait*

                   *for the Messiah. We waited like crazy*
                        *monkeys, half-skeleton, half-monkey,*

                             *sheared heads,  screaming*
                                  *the Viddui prayer, shaking*

*the walls of the gas chamber. Except*
         *for your Aunt Aliza. What she said*

                   *if I translate to English, is like,*
                        *'We're not going yet.'*

                             *Morning was snow and sun together*
                                  *with changed orders:*

*'Out from the gas chamber,*
         *walk to the next camp.' Auschwitz. Who knew*

                   *Auschwitz would save us?*
                        *It needed more numbers, more arms for numbers.*

                             *So we counted*
                                  *for something.*

# HAWKS

I jog up a switchback and spot the two clumps
of jonquils popped open at the base of Weeping Rock
from which just last month icicles hung
like unsheathed glistening sabers.

My face flushes pink as a piglet. I feel solid and bright.
It's more than a runner's high. It's winter's fecund destruction.
The necessity of it. I bound over downed trees, squash
spongy chartreuse moss that grows in damp patches

as ice sheets retreat. A red-tailed hawk lands,
impossibly heavy for the branch, like the TV
on the too-small shelf of my childhood
kitchen where we watched the bad news

settle in the Bay of Pigs and stayed
tuned, out of necessity, for Carol Burnett's slap-
stick, how she'd slosh the forlorn mop, find her
foot stuck in a blue bucket, how at the end

of the hour, somehow, she'd yank it out, then pull
on her left earlobe to signal to her grandmother
that she had once again triumphed over her own
demise. Each week we'd watch yet again for the sign

that we too were safe from destruction.
In the woods I watch the hawk blend into bark,
lift off, float. I never see the pounce. A red-tail
once got its head caught in a crisscross of fence

by our house and we watched for hours its frantic
flapping, listened to its shrieks and scary silences.
The guy from the bird sanctuary wore hunter-
green suede gloves as he worked the bird's head,

wheedled it from the diamond shape, wrapped
the stunned creature in a plaid blanket, shot it full
of steroids to make the brain-swell subside,
held it close, put it in the back seat, offered

only a guarded prognosis. In swaddled stillness,
the hawk's feathers fluffed up like a plush robe,
extravagant hair. My mother never looked
calm like that, never dressed in a robe or fluffed

out her hair. During the Bay of Pigs, she bought
cans and cans of food, blankets of varying weights,
built a closet in the basement to hold them,
and watched like a hawk for signs of destruction.

## SHIVA: GOD OF MERCY, GOD OF DESTRUCTION

How the taut strings of the instrument,
how the wood, how the shine of the wood,
how the years of care, how the dryness
that needs to be moistened,
how the wet of your patient mouth,
how the memory of the first time
your mouth found its way,

how the thought of not being,
how the thought of being only
one, how the leanness of bodies, of legs,
how your legs wrap my legs,
how bellies, how backs, how thighs
tauten, how the length of
days stretches and shortens behind us,

deep copper curtains, how trees
enter the room, how sky
also enters. Hungry
ghosts enter, how still,
I bid them stay
though they say they are up
to no good. How strong their desire,
how subversive the lure. The crash

of shadows on walls.
How to send the ghosts
to their own beds
with no supper, how to know
they will be hungry.
How they will never believe
they are already dead.

## SAYING YOUR NAME

*Saying your name colors my mouth,*
*frees loose this river, changes my skin,*
*turns my spine to string. I pray all the time now.*
*Amen.*          —Patricia Smith

It is true that when, in the cayenne-colored
kitchen, you touch my ankle and trail
your fingers up my calf, maybe to feel how
strong the muscle or how dry the skin, I imagine

us on the cumin-colored spread, your ginger fingertips
tripping along my ribs and ridge of clavicle until
you are inside and outside my skin at the same time,
until you are licking the tips of your fingers

preparing to play in the moist clouds of my body,
and when you are inside the clouds, I can see all
the pulsing lights of planes in flight that look
like they are only still—stars blinking.

Sometimes our soaring reminds me of ways I,
we, couldn't love, failed to love years ago
before our hair turned silver. If I am lucky
I remember the woods we walk and the woman

who lives there with no regrets, no failures, no history
in the sheets of mica schist, in garnet-studded boulders.
Her impartial eyes gaze out from faces
of deep trees, heavy-bodied-white-tailed deer,

steep slopes and strapping rain,
rocks and stones that emerge
from the ground after so many years
of our stumbling.

## PICTURE OVER THE EDGE

Above my desk gladiolas
re-open every morning
thick and oily on the five-
by-five foot canvas, too big
to be buried with. Some days
violet, other days vermilion
grabs me by the throat. Tight
green buds show
no signs of which color
will reveal itself
in the morning. No one can say,
not even the experts,
whether the gladiola-
shaped mass with its tissue-
thin petals, folded-
open, is made merely of dead
tissue, or cells dangerously blooming.
Why not go a little crazy?
Open, close, open, shake and shake
the painting like a kaleidoscope,
jumble the little chips of light
so much that everything turns
to shards of beauty
and no sad story
can stick.

## DANCE OF THE CRANES

In our bed you licked the rose
oil and bergamot from my legs
that lengthened and heated in the mercy
of your tongue and feather touch.

But not today. Today glaring yellow, neon green,
audacious orange origami cranes, a flock of them,
shimmy and jive in the inciting breeze across the jasmine-
scented bedroom filled with fear.

Pass a pin through the head to make the eye.
Feed the thread through the eye to tether each crane
to the other, a chorus-line of jolts and jitter.
To win over his mate, the male crane kicks

high, hops, whips his wings in a wild fouette
while standing on one leg, then bows with a flourish.
High above marshlands in the Black Mountains
of Bhutan, black-necked cranes circle clockwise

three times over the snow and walls and roof
of the monastery before swooping down to rebuild
their homes. All year the monks pray for safe return
of the winged Bodhisattvas who live twice

as long as the Bhutanese, and it is believed
they fly into each incarnation knowing
every dance necessary for joy.
Cranes mate for life. The dance seals their bond.

This is the one with whom they'll bleed
last blood, whoop over their young
and before battle as long beaks poke
the sweet spot at the temple of their prey.

Tonight, you step onto the dance floor
for the first time in months. Your long arms spread
open like the porte-de-bras of the ocean-blue crane,
fingers drape like a crystal waterfall. Rushing

behind you, a flock of fellow dancers shadows
your signature scoop and twirl, reassured
nothing essential for joy has been taken
from you and therefore from themselves.

So long you have done the dance of the crane,
have tethered yourself to earth and my love.
Tomorrow you must trust the connecting thread
to pull you through the dark eye of the needle.

## OPEN, SHE SAYS


Jumping up and down as if on a springboard
        faster and faster she begs
                the musicians to play      her mouth

she says must stay open as her body
        can only jump with her mouth
                open she says

                        like the dead
                                or the child in wonder
                                        we must all

        dance she says
                so no one can tell us
                        apart      she can't

stop jumping and I hate that
        I need her
                body and mouth

                        to stay open
                                so I can shut
                                        my door

        or leave it
                open just a crack
                        for light

                        it takes so long
                                to learn to leave
                                        room for light

## JUMP

Six teenaged boys jump off the bridge
into the creek thirty feet below. Shivering,
they hike back onto the wall, squat for some seconds
before each plunge. Blue and green tattoos of skulls
or girls swell on ripped calves. I like watching them
shiver, jump, free themselves from fear for the moment.

A skinny blond girl says, *Yeah, I dove in
headfirst last week*, which everyone knows
must be a lie, though no one calls her on it.
The boys wear sneakers except for one
who clasps a small rock with his toes.
It's as if he has talons. He looks prideful, happy.

I wish the shortest guy luck, the one still dry,
and walk over the bridge and deep among wide
and narrow trees, upturned and down-driven roots.
Daily death catches in our teeth. Daily I cook the soft
boiled eggs, stand on the bridge, pretend to not be
watching for the tumor to re-grow. Daily I long

for my beloved to smash the crystal turtle, toss
the tusked elephant, trunk turned ever upward,
hurl the hunk of healing amethyst, rip the *Life
beyond Cancer* book, long for him to hide
his fear that his immune system will fail him
if he kisses me, shivering.

## FOR EXAMPLE

Take the seasons, for example,
how they drift imperviously,
impersonally, toward their own
demise, flowering or beating
in the wind, budding or breaking
apart. Take snow, how steadily
it falls on the upper ridge, how it
heaps on hives and nests,
prances in patterns on tree barks
like waltzers dotting or crowding
on vertical dance floors. Take,
for example, the flakes,
how they burrow into grooves
of fallen oak and ash, ringed trunks
that lie helter-skelter on the hill
just below the ridge, where
the sound of the creek and
the stories of the creek
are soundless though you
hear them with your eyes. Take
for example the wide view
from the ridge; you see nothing
that looks out of place, as if
you're looking at a topographic
map of exact chaos.

Take, for example, the Heart
that is not yours alone
to suffer and love.

## THE VEIL

gets thinner and we get

more tactile, touching more and more, touching

both sides.

Don't ask me

why I wasn't afraid; ask the years

I didn't know the woods

would lift me.

## ON HIS PALM

she draws a window,
cracks it open. The grey egg-
shaped rock she places
on the ledge
of his palm.

A black stain,
irregularly shaped, covers the face
of the rock that will sit
on edge.

The African woman
who sold her the rock
said that in her village
of rocks no one would
buy a rock, especially
one burdened with
the word *hope*.

The saleswoman urged her
to choose another
rock, one with
no stain. What
would be the point of *hope*
carved on a rock
with no stain?

The word *hope* disturbs her
today as she has places it
on the ledge
of the window
left wide open.

Today they will pinpoint
the spot that will burn
for the next six weeks,
daily, exactingly, radiantly.

## STUDIO BLUES

More pink than I had hoped—
pink is not really my color,
perhaps just the deepest
tones augment
my mood, and yet it was all
I could paint—all
over the rasping coarseness
of these stucco walls that let in
the cold but still
remind me of the Southwest
where every day
colors excited, crazed, did me in—
nothing in this high-ceilinged
studio, except the six-foot
triangular window, eye
to eye with the one remaining
evergreen whose top towers
over our three story
house, nothing
in this high-ceilinged room
distracts or entices
except perhaps the lone
vase that stands on wide-board pine—
no sense of what made me
buy that vase, its shape
not unusual, and yet the day I chose it
my darling held
his nose against the mold
smells of the barn and vowed
to stay with me
this once for a shopping seduction,

he usually refuses, as he's prone
to headaches caused by getting lost
in the fruit aisle
at the Acme, or was it the
soldier aisle at ToysRUs,
for how long, no one recalls
it the same way, as is always the case,
but now that we know
how much is at stake—a gilded
trap door we fall through—
the vase, the vase—

## PRAYIN' WOMAN

Grateful to be awake, I call Verizon and get Victoria, the specialist in matters of cancellation. Actually, first I get Paul the non-specialist who says, *I am giving you to Vicki, I mean Victoria.* Vicki is peeved with Paul for his informality. *My name is Miss McCree. Mr. Pratt has explained your whole situation,* which means Paul has told Vicki about my desire to cancel the business line due to my husband's illness, his cancer; now I just call it that, though the whole tumor supposedly was burned away, still he takes those little chemo pills which cause a smoldering or a reeking kind of fear, depending on the host's response to unwelcome change. Surely those pills say something very different than *the cancer's all gone.*

*May I inquire, ma'am, are you a prayin' woman?* asks Miss McCree, which catches me off guard, makes me weep a bit and feel glad of it; crying with strangers is the only time I cry these days though I used to be a great crier anywhere, would have made quite a good living running in circles around the amphitheater, wailing and renting black garments as Orestes or Agamemnon lay still in the center of the stage.

I thank Verizon's Victoria for reminding me I am a prayin' woman, though I don't say to whom I pray. She responds, *Don't thank me. Thank the Lord. He speaks through me.* I thank her for being open to the Lord speaking through her. She can't refuse that gratitude.

I cry to the checkout lady at Wal-Mart, though I know it is politically incorrect to shop there; I cry with the bank manager not because she can help me but because her husband just died and still she says God is good all the time; anyone who says God is good all the time, I cry to. The Structure sales clerk, a middle-aged Asian woman I like very much, how careful she is when she folds and unfolds the sweater I will bring home for my husband. We will cut open the back to make it like a warm hospital gown. So many losses I can't hold on to.

Last week a nun sat beside me on the plane back from Hartford who saw the book in my hands and wanted to hear about my parents' Holocaust stories, mother's Auschwitz saga, and father's clothes rotting off his body in the living grave. Suddenly I realized how I grew up in celebrity lighting, brighter than Greek tragedy, stories of God working miracles, that is, if you focused on successes of my parents at staying alive.

*Why you keep writing about the Holocaust? So many years ago it was, we went through this, not you. Your father, so sick these past six years, he is my Holocaust now.* That's what Momma used to say. I never knew how to answer her until now: Holocaust horrors always kept their distance yet called and called to me. Captivating, clean, mine but not mine. Now I write of my beloved's illness and the story is mine and not mine. I draft a letter for my husband that says, *Dear valued patients, Thank you for the opportunity ... over 30 years...I have decided...for personal reasons...to close the doors of my holistic medical practice...* nothing about the little pills, the awake craniotomy.

*And you, how have you been?* Friends ask me. I don't tell them I have been hoarding things, the huge lavender linen jacket and matching skirt I bought maybe twenty years ago to hide my body in the years I wasted on worry about a square inch tag in the neckline of a dress, the number printed on it, and the bigger numbers that moved ever so slightly on a scale. Now, I go up and down on the numbers of items I place in the Purple Heart bags. In the end I miss their house call and am glad of it. I don't want to give anything else away. My darling's eyes are puffy and hollow. The tiny blue pills come in white bottles that take two people to open. Red pills next month. Each month stronger doses come in hotter colors on the color wheel while my dear one appears to be any one of the 72 shades of white.

I put ads in the paper for help. I get Miss Sylvene, a black Baptist who runs her own ministry in her God-given house up the street, says, *God, He give us the one tool we need for this Life and we keep looking for a brighter, faster, better one. But woman, there be no better tool.* She means, of course, the tool of prayer and I am puzzled as to why I keep finding myself among preachin' women, prayin' women.

I go to the beauty salon just to feel the hands of Miss Ernestine, my favorite hair washer who rubs the back of my neck real slow in the right spots around the bones and says, *You keep listenin', honey. The Lord spoke through a rock, a bush, a donkey.*

## CALL AND RESPONSE

*Then Moses said, 'Now show me your glory.' And God said, 'I will
cause all my goodness to pass in front of you, but you cannot see my
face, for no one may see me and live. I will put you in a cleft in the
rock and cover you with my hand until I have passed by.'*
                                                    —Exodus 33:19, 18-23


And you shall love
the rock and the cleft

of the rock from which I call to you,
in which I hide my face

inside your face. Our eyes
view the close land and the lands

beyond the close land. You will paint
white the trunks of young avocado trees

to keep them from the sun's burning.
You will you pluck pears from the pear trees

for they will not ripen otherwise. Even so,
famine and devastation will visit every land.

May it all be for you one holy pilgrimage.
Focus on the light or the darkness

behind your eyes or the mixture of the two.
Rest in the certainty

that you will be swallowed up, *betul ha yesh,*
into the *annihilation of somethingness,*

that you will turn to endless eyes
that survey every land, measure every need

for darkness. Until then you will endure
and weep with gladness that you have found

in the cleft of the rock, your face,
my face, together in the dark.

## WHEN YOU BECOME SNOW

When you become snow, Love,
fresh fallen or later black ice
on the path by the river
when you become the river
and the silty bottom of the river
when the water becomes
you and also flows over you
when the river freezes in some places
and stays fluid in others and spider
patterns haunt the icy channels,
you won't need to ask the river
if you are not only the marrow
that fills the hollow
but also the transparent skin
on the face of God.

## HOW DO YOU LOVE YOUR LIFE?

Though you cannot rescue yourself
from the weight or shift of sands,
pour emerald into every desert.

Desert hills on their haunches,
always on the ready, cannot separate
themselves from the mountain's solitude

no matter how distant lies the mountain.
In the desert, bone-white dust storms.
The territory of emptiness fills you.

No hidden lakes in the desert.
On the mountain, the weightless
lift away, lift away.

## MAGICAL THINKING

*If it dies before I get to you—*
*if I set it free and it flies off—*
*if I lift the lid and it falters—*
*you will die before I reach you—*
*or you will definitely*
*not die today.*

I park. As if on cue
the butterfly goes crazy,
flaps, flutters. I walk.
This is how magical
thinking works. I pull
off the paper towel.

Butterfly zooms straight up
into the great blue day.
It leaves me with nothing
up my sleeve.
I come to you
empty-handed.

## NO ONE SPEAKS

of these intimacies
when the dying say,
*I cannot help you any more,*
and the living say, *I know,*
but don't really
mean it, and a panic
arises
in the living
never before felt
except perhaps
when a child awakens
in the night and the cry
is not yet a cry
and the child licks
and sucks the air and finds
not a drop of sweet,
not because the mother
doesn't want to give
her breast but because
in that moment
the house is silent,
dark and intimate
as the moon.

## TRANSPORT

When the transport team carried you
covered with four flimsy hospital blankets

on the slatted gurney up the walkway
to the front of our Dutch Colonial

you whispered, *Stop*. Our son heard.
I, lagging behind, didn't.

The men held the hard handles
for a long time as you took your

last look at our home from the outside,
saw September, the smoke bushes deep purple.

Doors and windows, opening and closing.
Then they carried you inside.

## JOHNSON OR UPSAL

I can't remember if the ambulance guy
drove up Johnson, the way I told him,

or Upsal, the way you whispered he should go
as you lay in the truck strapped to a slatted gurney.

I'd like to think I let you have your way.
But the only thing I can say for sure is

sometimes I needed something
to make me feel powerful.

# PART II

## IN THE BARDO OF DYING

You look far off into a place I cannot go or see.
You say, *We are nothing but millions and millions of stars.*
Your mouth is open like a child

with the first taste of sky.

~

You say you see Van Gogh's Starry Night.
How thick and yellow the moon, how blue
the hills and wind.

I say, *How present the mountain.*

⸬

You say you have been thinking about the Hell realms.
How quickly they pass. *One thought brings suffering.*
*Let it pass. Another thought, suffering. Let it pass.*

You are already part of the mountain.

~

Each day you live through makes me
forget we all die. Makes me close
my heart. Let it break

tomorrow.

~

You look onto puffs of purple smoke
bushes you planted last fall. Tufted air
mattress you lie on, fills and releases—

fills and releases.

~

You laugh often these days.
I say, *I am glad you are able to laugh.*
You say, *I hope you get to laugh too.*
I say, *You mean now?*

Your mouth forms a perfect *O*
as you say, *Noooo,*
*when it's your turn,*
*when it's your turn!*

~

Instead of words today
I bring you a handful of red
berries, tiny, shining,
and a palm-shaped piece

of bark, five holes drilled
in a row. 960 times
per minute the woodpecker
hammers praises into the trees.

~

You say, *I don't know who we are.*
I know this is meant to be a Zen koan
seated in the unknown. But since I am
of the Jewish tradition of commentary,

and though I too don't know who we are,
I say, *We are shooting stars, dust arcing*
*even as I transform into fields of tall grasses*
*and you into groves of fruit trees.*

~

Head tilts back.
Face feels sunlight.
Body feels water.
Arms feel lip

of cement coping.
Stay inside my own body.
Lie beside my beloved.
Stay inside my own body.

~

The last of ten ox-herding pictures.
I never until now saw how
the empty moon
has swallowed up the boy

and the ox and the thousands
of trees and valleys.
No shadows
at night, no shadows.

## AS THE MOON HAS BREATH

Ordinary, plain, neither lonely nor not lonely
or whatever is the opposite of lonely.
Life without you is not life without you.

In the photo, you breathe from inside
the mountain, emerge like a lotus flower,
palms open, bright sun inhabits your face.

In your dying months I saw you stripped
of idiosyncrasies, defenses,
accomplishments, embellishments.

I saw your essence, not like pure rain,
more like different kinds of wind.
Maybe it is simple like the breath

that begins us, ends us. Maybe you were
simply breath, as the ocean has breath,
as the night sky has breath, as the moon has breath.

## NOW THE SMOKE BUSHES

We agreed we had no more to say
as we sat face to face, your left ear
pointing heavenward. Left equals language,

I bring myself to recall how *round*
meant *hard*, how I was the only one
who could decipher

aphasia's lexicon
when you said,
*the egg is cold and round,*

and finally I said,
*I think you mean cold and hard,*
though I did not move

to make a soft and hot egg,
So it was like that.
How the round sad hard

soft-boiled egg lay
stuck to the bottom of the pot
brought upstairs

by the hired help who
had been trying to re-heat it,
or maybe she was tired

of trying, as I was,
to do anything more
to please a dying man.

⁓

Now seven months after your body
was sung into the earth
I think of the afternoon I put the spoon

in your mouth too quickly
wanting only to catch the last
rays of sun and you smiled and whispered,

*Five more minutes,*
and so I blew on the broth
for what I foolishly hoped was

enough time
to spare me
from regrets.

⁓

Three a.m. snack. I swear I hear you
call my name from upstairs.
But I dismiss it

not because you are dead
but because you would never
be up at this hour.

⁓

*You look tired,* you had said to me
as I placed the bright pink sponge
to your lips for you to suck on.

It made me so happy you saw me
that day with tender eyes,
intimate, complete.

~

Rib cage like wire, like balsa, like tabla.
Breaths, ten per minute. I thought it would be
easier for me once you were gone

to wake and write and breathe
to let the sun fill the earth and give off
its loamy essence from our hillside.

Instead I make you alive though I do not
picture us reliving anything—
not swimming side by side

in the turquoise sea year after year,
not planting the purple smoke bushes
months before your diagnosis. They are now

eight feet high and you are missing
the tufts that look like billowing filigree
smoke. They dazzle and burn the living.

## EMBRACE

To bear loss
nothing
must be unutterable
the words you say
will not leave your lips
as you intend
the moment will not appear
as you imagined
as you braced for
you must embrace
sea-deep emptiness
you are made from
dust and trust
as the stars
as brilliant
as dead
as alive
as they

## DUST-WHITE

The night you visited me
after you died, Poppa, the sun
shone on your bald head and you were wearing
your most lively smile, and a swirling
blue-green spiral for a body.
*Remember the colors,*
you said. And when I awoke

I hiked up to the ridge
just past Weeping Rock,
sat on the bench carved,
*Wish you were here,*
saw the blue-green spruces spinning
their blue-green spirals and felt at ease,
assured those were the colors you meant.

Now the old bench boards
have blown away.
No more wishes.
I rub my fingers over
and over the new rosewood
engraved with the name
of my beloved—

*He is a portion*
*of the loveliness*
*which once he made*
*more lovely—*
look out onto lively
limbs of a distant sycamore,
sturdy trunk, dust-white bark,

white dust of bark,
feel his thick, yet nimble,
thumb to index, thumb to middle,
as he sprinkles the dust–
white, which means all
colors of the earth,
onto my arms.

## ABOUT THE MAGNESIUM CAPSULES YOU
## SWORE SOOTHED THE NERVOUS SYSTEM
## INTO SLEEP

No one witnesses my life.
No one calls upstairs when I don't
come down to dinner in the ten
minutes I said I would, asking
exactly which version of ten
minutes I am employing tonight.
No one chides me when the rice
cakes crunch in my mouth in the king-
sized bed, no one wears that cheeky
grin as he slides apart
three magnesium caps, shakes loose
the powder into his mouth,
makes certain some of its white
dust lands on his lips and chin
just to see me roll and bat
my eyes at the same time,
just to hear me whisper,
*Oh, darling, how attractive,*
just to feel my fingertips
against his petulant chin
and all along the pucker,
press and open of his lips
as I brushed the dust away.

## SHE WILL CIRCLE

Even on a bright endless day
she will circle the cool corner
of the room and curl into a whimper.

She will pull on her clunky boots,
unleashed and fetch the morning newspaper
still addressed to the dead.

## BEST OFFER

A friend calls to offer
advice. I want none.
Humility is the best offer
to widows. Also, berries, or a zebra-
striped robe to wear outdoors
so the widow can blend in,
as zebras do,
with the wavy lines
of tall grasses
against a wild horizon.

## LOST IS NOT A PLACE

Lost is not a place I have been unless
you count the places on your body
I have touched with the palms of my hands.

Lost is not a place unless I look for you
in the pale blue sweater folded in the closet,
and the black and white checkered

one with the zipper up the front, that one
too, or in the uneven footprints in the carpet.
Lost is not a place I have been unless

you believe me when I say: I can bear this,
I can, if I keep the middle drawer closed,
and the closet door too, for today, I can.

## *YOU ARE MY LIONESS*

How did you hunt down
the exact words to feed me
the courage to get you

out of hospice?
For seven nights I bit
into rare meat

to ready myself
for your breath
stopping in the same

room where I had laid
my head on your thigh
just below

your pelvic bone,
your heart beating
everywhere.

## RED DRESS

There is a red dress every woman has worn,
longed for, eschewed, slipped from,
left hanging, her hair, every woman
has tied back with ribbons, practiced,
every woman, lips against

looking glass. Momma practices
her lips on shapely red
Jell-O that wiggles inside the clear
plastic container, as rust-
colored iron flows, thick and slow,

through a transparent tube into
her body. Breaking apart
the soft white bread, dry turkey,
I offer only a ragged
half-slice instead of the two pieces

placed in the box alongside the red
Jell-O. These days, Momma eats only
what is given to her, the way Poppa did,
the way my darling did,
near the end. *100 Questions to Ask*

*Your Mother,* I read to Momma:
*Was your childhood home noisy or quiet?*
*Dark or bright?* Momma is happy
she knows the answers and adds
how she often stole

a look, over the low partition,
at the boarders: the man who smelled
of strong perfume, and his wife who hollered,
*Hanina, don't leave me*
*without money for the butcher.*

*Tell me about your red dress.*
There are questions every woman
has left hanging on points
of an endless chain-link
fence that surrounds

and separates every-mother
every-daughter, no matter
how close or far away, any woman can hear
the rustle of red dresses, the reverb
of metal mesh being shaken and shaken.

## LONG HALL

*The world of matter is a relative world, an illusory one; illusory
not in the sense that it does not exist, but in the sense that we
do not see it as it really is..... dancing energy and transient
impermanent forms.*      —Gary Zukav


Now that I too am in the long-haul
practice of care-giving, I need to ask
if you think it useful to memorize
the impermanent shape of their ears?
To become that familiar
with another would take
a lifetime of mirrors.

I feel the touch and press
of unseen energies. How far
will I trust the unknown? The force
that pushed our hands across
the Ouija board, how suddenly
we are arrived

on the other side of the board, giddy,
pinkies touching, friendship sealed,
both of us feeling forces
beyond us, but more
importantly, kindred
hands touching.

Here in the long hall the nurses
are relieved we have signed the DNR
order for our mother. After all she is so close
to ninety and has outlived so many.
Then there is this reality:

she is lying on the gurney saying,
*I still want to make it to the b'nai mitzvah*
*of the twins,* which you know
is one year away, and there is this:
when the nurse asks momma
what month it is,

she smiles and answers,
*I know it's almost March,*
which it is not, but you know
March is the month that
will celebrate
six family birthdays
including her own,

and so it is the only month
of the year that matters
other than May,
her son's birthday. No other months
have meaning to her, no other months
contain the dancing particles of the universe.

## WAIT

*for Momma*


Of dense forests
of clothing, monogrammed towels,
nightgowns that carry
your smells, calendula and Lancôme
dusting powder, I say,
*Take it, take it,*
*no wait, wait, I cannot walk*
*so quickly through this*
*shaking room*
*empty of you, full of you.*

I have tossed
all the sucking candies, giant
round tins full of them
for your throat
clearing and clearing,
your holding to life, even
in the white room
when I said to the aide
just six hours before your death,
*I know you're not happy*

*to stay the night here*
*instead of at the house,*
and you thought I was speaking to you,
so you answered, *Who says I'm not happy?*
*I'm happy. I'm happy I'm alive.*
Then, to the girl in line ahead of you
for the MRI just two hours
before your death, you said,
*So young you are dear,*
*why are you here, so late it is?*

How you smiled, not a fake smile,
through the *Twelfth of Never*
I found necessary to sing to you
in the white hallway
as you lay under four slight
white blankets warmed in the same
ER-warmer that warmed
my beloved's blankets
just four months before.

Now I stand in your apartment
taking photos of each corner
of each immaculate room,
sunlight pouring through.
Your dark glasses still resting
on the coffee table. Photos
for the couple with three
toddlers halfway across
the globe, who wish
to rent ASAP, but then
I stop and say to no one,
*Wait, wait, I want*
*the Farberware back.*
Someone took your shiny pots
before I could say,
*Farina and double-strained*
*carrot-sweet chicken soup.*
*Wait, wait.* They say
it will be one hundred
degrees today, yet the air
in here is cold
and smells of almost snow.

## WOMAN WHO PULLS

How often I see her
the woman who pulls
her own hair and screams
in the far left corner—
she could
take over
if I paid her
any mind. I do
keep track of her
as she is the one
I believe I could be
all the time,
grief plundering
as it wants,
were it not for the steady
pulse of the sea,
red-billed tropicbird
that runs up and down
the white-foam corridor, stops
ten feet from me, stares with one
yellow eye, one black
unblinking center.

## MIRRORS

Daily he told me I was beautiful,
my breast cupped in his palm cured
me of any doubt. So you see why

I cannot gaze at my own nakedness.
Mirrors tell you nothing about love.
The tilted fir outside my window

stands taller than our house. Even if
I described each tuft, counted
branches to become its mirror,

you could never love it as I do,
understand how it kept me faithful,
stood watch with me when the other tree fell.

## AND STILL SWOOP ME UP

For weeks before your death the Zen master
guides you through a meditation on *hearing
rest, seeing rest, feeling rest* to prepare you

to be swallowed up
by the ever spinning sphere
of expansion and contraction.

After the first meditation, he asks how you feel.
You say, *Relieved. How come I am a butterfly
going and coming, coming and going?*

The Zen master says, *That sounds very good.*
You say to me, *Remember that.* You flutter
your fingers toward and away from your heart.

~

Thirty days after your death an orange
and black monarch hovers over my knee
as I stand in woods we walked for thirty years.

But it's not you. Nor are you the yellow-
breasted finch that lands overhead.
You are the lavender

cloud that grabs hold
of the setting sun and steals
its light for me.

~

Forty-nine days after your death
the Buddhists believe you enter
your next incarnation. I try to believe

your soul can enter another body
and still swoop me up
night after night, shove me

out of my mental chatter,
remind me
how short our days.

## THE SPIRIT WATCHERS

When I said the *shomrim* would keep
watch over your body for twenty-four

hours after you died so your spirit
would be quickly freed, you shrugged,

whispered, *No need, I'll go,*
*phew, like that!* You snapped

your fingers. *Want to know why?*
You asked. *Because I don't want*

*to be cold!* Your smile, triumphant,
emphatic. Every day, still,

you challenge me
to get more spacious, let more

and more of my strength in, let
more and more of your spirit leave.

## PINE ARMOIRE

If we had not had a history of disagreeing about the pine
armoire, my solo bargain purchase, you wishing someone
would just cart it away, *Please, anyone, take it,*

you'd say to guests, you'd even pay for movers,
if we had not sat side-by-side on camelback couches
and Queen Anne love seats for two years and twenty

stores to choose the one that didn't give you
a backache and didn't make my neck feel too long,
if we could have agreed during our three decades

and more, on even the height of a footstool,
I would never have known the grievous
pleasure of giving in to your taste for clove-

colored low-pile carpet and suede-to-match
headboard, bureau with manly bulk, brushed
silver drawer-pulls, dark wood, clean lines.

No more floral chintzes anywhere. No more
your feathery fingers on my chest and neck;
I gave away all my flowers for you

and yet you left me shaking
down all the furniture, making the nightstand
pay for my loss; I open and slam shut its drawers.

I've frankly had my fill of having my way
with the Victorian stuffed cushions; I'm taking on
your taste for sparseness; sometimes I simply sit inside

the armoire because I love to remember how you
enjoyed hating it and because I need to be held
by its heaviness.

## LIE DOWN

When I ask how
he's feeling, he says
lonely, missing

the shelter of being
his father's son.
When he calls me

into his room all legs, boyhood
and manhood under the old quilt,
when he motions for me to lie down

beside him, when I lie down
beside him, when I hold back
all words, a bright silence

presses my cheek
against his cheek,
spreads over the place

in each of us
that feels homeless,
harmed.

## INVINCIBLE

From his fridge he grabs the family-sized jar of mayo
though he lives alone with only Manhattan's perfect
electricity shooting in all directions. Ninety miles away,

she puts the red porcelain kettle on blue flames that burst
like a dangerous flower. He entered the world with his heart,
they said, beating too slowly, maybe the cord caught

in the curve of his neck, so they flipped her body,
drained of all fluids, over and back again three times
in hopes of shaking him out, she, cursing the Lamaze ladies

who said labor would be just that and nothing more,
the night-shift doctor cursing the day-shift doctor
who went off duty without prepping knives,

the baby's headlong descent finally cut open
quick and angry. The new father laid his head
on the new mother's belly, declined to cut the cord,

wept for the baby's beauty, aliveness, and his own
father's too-young last words, just two weeks before,
*I could ride forever.* At home the new mother put

the baby in the sunlight on the living room carpet
and he'd stay there for hours basking until his fine hair
was warm and bleached golden and his eyes loved her

as if she had kept her promise. When he was a boy
she used the yellow crayon to color-in He-man's
suit of armor that stretched across his chest to make him

invincible. Tonight she pictures Manhattan's blue
subway seats the day she rushed to grab three
side-by-side, how father and son had laughed.

Below the son's third floor walk-up,
3 a.m. cabbies would be turning roof lights on, or off.
*I could ride forever. I could ride forever.*

She remembers all the nights her son cradled
his father's head against his chest
hoping to make him invincible.

# LAST LETTER

Ghalib, the storm
will be your resting place. Its eye will be your watchman.
Your mourning rites will lead to your freedom.
Your love for this world will leak out, drop-by-drop,
until you are all love turned inside out.

Cloud in the eye
will be your father, sun in the eye will be your
teacher, woman in white walking with woven
basket balanced on her head, will hold
your fortune, strange and sumptuous fruit.

Ghalib, I hear you
will journey to a distant land where the teacher
is as ready as the student, where you will give
everything you know away, where your arms
will open like the petals of a lotus flower.

I will not be watching.
I will not be the bindi on the forehead of the guru's wife.
In the photo she looks happy and the guru also.
It is said he cured a king
and saved a plainsman.

The guru, if he is a good one,
will teach you the song you wrote in your dream,
and bind you with what you wish for and what you
dread, connection without loss, connection that risks
losing everything.

Weep with oneness
as you find yourself to be another. Carry your love
of thunder and drum, fresh basil and brown rice, thick fog
that rolled in suddenly on Mt. Tam
when we traveled together.

Go gladly, Ghalib,
with your new tribe of hot sands, metal drum.
Tribe of your heart, broken and whole, welcomed and lonely,
beating like the sun-
yellow wings of the Bugun bird.

Such is love, Ghalib,
what we dread and wish for are the same. I begin again and again to
write to you before I pass from this earth
into her moist darkness, earth that pours the seas and rivers
into my waiting mouth.

# PART III

## TELL ME I AM BEAUTIFUL

Click-click—the grass grows, won't stop—the wind blows—in the night when birds fluff feathers round necks and you are not here to tuck myself into, no matter how small the world gets, and the grass grows taller in this perfect month of September, when I am to travel to Sicily, home of the Mafia and medieval towns crumbling; maybe that is why I can't bring myself to go; so much lies in ruin.

Tourists click-click on high stone walls that grow green mold, while Italian men whistle and make lewd remarks no matter what a woman's age, though at my age it may be worth the ten-hour plane ride to hear someone tell me I am beautiful. I hear Erice is a town where you can never get lost, as all the cobblestone streets lead back to wherever you began. Grateful, I am, for the chance to travel, but not for the reality of it. I'd rather stay lost here in the turn of the woods, on the hill I last walked with you, in the garden where your utterly goofy sunhat gave shade even to the crabgrass.

## PUT THE FLAME IN THE SHOWER

Three full moons after your death, on a Sunday, exactly at noon, Mara called to ask permission to send three angels to our house, angels guaranteed to grant me three wishes.

*Could they be latchkey angels?* I asked, since I knew I'd be very busy that Sunday stirring my cauldron in my debut performance as Shaman of Cups, high priestess of Tarot, and the boiling contents would be viscous, and it would take all my strength to stir.

Mara made it clear: *The angels are not permitted to unlock doors by themselves. You must not only be home when they arrive, but you'll need to prepare, place your three wishes inside an envelope along with a list of ten people to whom the angels will fly for the next ten Sundays. And when the clock strikes noon, you must trust they have arrived, say a welcome prayer, and light a special candle that will burn for seven days and nights.*

It's been four full moons since that Sunday and I haven't had the heart to say to Mara, *Sorry but I just couldn't let in the angels.* I'd have to explain how I am about houseguests, how we both were, how, on purpose, we never had a spare bed for anyone, and how I can't bear to make wishes that might not come true, or ones that might. What reason would I have, then, for any future unhappiness?

Besides, Momma taught me never to leave a candle burning any place but in the shower. So if I put the flame in the shower for seven days and nights, how would I manage a morning without feeling your fingers lather the pearly purple shampoo into my hair? I can't tell her that though I live alone now, the house is way too crowded.

## INSTEAD OF ANGELS

For every brain tumor I hear about—for every morning my own brain can't balance out its darkness with enough *amens* and *blessed bes*—for every evening I can't be my own comforting community—I need a white wing to enfold me. But as I've already explained, I couldn't let in the angels, so I decided to try a bereavement group where in the small rectangular office, seated around a large rectangular table, we all waited in strained silence for the group leader to arrive.

To pass the time, I colored in my nametag with the turquoise and yellow markers strewn on the table by the group leader. Another widow with one cross-eye that stayed stuck by the bridge of her nose, as if waiting for courage to cross, who sported a pair of thick white winged glasses, said, *Oh, you're already doing well. They say if you use color you're doing well, really well.*

I rolled the turquoise marker toward her, the one called *Swelling Sea* before I noticed *Purple-Mountain-Majesty* lay untouched on her end of the table. No other widow seated at the table was willing to pick up any color.

Perhaps they were afraid of the evil eye that surely comes to those who appear to be *doing well.* Or maybe no one wanted the blue flames of their marriage to ignite or die down, the green hills of their years together to roll any closer or further away, the red spikes of last days to impale them.

No one even wanted to color in the crocuses that had sprung up overnight—sun yellow, voluptuous violet, wedding white. Felicia, Rosanne, Ruthie, Sheila, Ayesha, I wanted to scream, *Play with me even though the sky is falling. Play with me because the sky is falling.* But I hadn't yet learned their names.

## *TO YOUR HEALTH*

You may, like me, have a whole day full of waiting in long lines at the Home Depot and Whole Foods Market the day before the January storm, and at home the cable box may, like mine, say, *no signal* and no one is there to help you, so you settle for being alive and you sit down at the table to bless your piece of turbot fish and your husband, saying, *to your health,* though he is dead five months now, still, his head tilts back as he inhales aromas of cumin and cardamom. You do try to remember you live alone, but it's foggy out, actually it's more like a huge mist covers your street, moist and shining.

## FIVE FULL MOONS

Daily I walk the woods alone, past the massive sycamore. Last night, a windstorm. Today the sycamore's hundreds of silver limbs lie across the valley, reminding me of the tangled tresses of Queen Isis cut off to mourn the slain king, her beloved Osiris, who lay in a golden coffin hidden in the hollow of a tree trunk. A squirrel searches bewildered, for its stockpile of acorns stored inside the sycamore. It stands silenced over the valley filled with grief no one wants to come close to. A week of black veils, a month of ripped black ribbon, a handful of walks in the woods with the widow. Enough.

It's been five full moons now. My phone doesn't ring anymore. Sound of the wind last night cracked me open. A week of black veils, a month of ripped black ribbons worn over the heart, a few long walks in the woods with the widow. Enough. Against all advice from well meaning friends, I opened my husband's spiral dream journal again, to the same page as last time, though no scrap of paper or folded corner marked the spot where he dreamed a tumor five years before its tendril roots appeared inside his brain and branched out so fast even the tearing night winds couldn't keep up.

This time I read further than the first time. In the dream our motherly friend Frances did the MRI of Steven's head even though he had gone in for a problem with his gallbladder. Also in the dream, or was it in his waking life, a squirrel entered the office through a crack in the wall and re-emerged soon after. The sneaking-in agitated him, the re-emergence saddened him; he writes he was sad for the squirrel. And for himself he wept and threw his body on the ground and felt afraid. In his dream I am not there to comfort him. I am not there to see the squirrel or the tumor breaking and entering.

In the backyard between our home and office, each year before the tumor, we watched for the one we called *the upside down squirrel* that found a way to chomp on thistle and niger seed from the bird feeder that hung from a branch of the star dogwood, no matter how we hung it, high, low, on thin wire or thick, on long or short rope. Last year we spray-painted its tail blue to be sure it was the same squirrel who kept returning, day after day, year after year, to keep us happy and complaining.

This year we didn't check for the upside-down squirrel's return nor did we speak of the mass shaped like two florets of a cauliflower. Weekly we went to the movies. In the last month of his life, at the last movie of his life, Steven sat between me and a stranger, a plump woman with thick thighs, who, midway through the film said, *Sir, I think your leg has fallen asleep on my leg.* I apologized, pulled his leg away, held it for the next hour as Susan Sarandon and Kate Winslet worked out a happy ending.

As the credits rolled I asked Steven, *Can you walk?* He said, *I think so, but maybe not tomorrow.* He didn't look at me, didn't weep or tear at the air, just rose slowly, and walked crooked and limpy, sat down on a bench outside the theater while I ran up five levels of painted yellow medial strip that divided the up-ramp from the down-ramp in the parking garage because I am afraid of elevators and because I needed some time to go crazy. To a man who needs to stay calm and needs his wife to stay equally calm, to a man who values equanimity, who needs hope that says his tree can withstand these hundred mile an hour winds, any snapping branches made him feel broken. To help him feel safe, I kept silent, nodded yes when he said he needed hope. Until it was time to say, *I have not lost hope but now I hope for different things: an easy death, a conscious death, a nothing-more-to-say death.*

Our son, who had come home for a month or was it two, fed him teaspoons of hot vegetable broth and chicken soup ice cubes, bent deep into his knees before lifting his father from the rented hospital bed into the king sized bed and back again, asked his father if he thought he'd be able to make a connection from the other world. Steven said, *Yes*. Our son said, *Me too*.

Most days I manage to keep out of the dream journal. Spring helps: yellow and purple crocuses, blue forget-me-nots, chipmunks, and dogs chasing chipmunks. Spring challenges: the garden without the man who planted everything here, the man who wept for the squirrel and for himself in the dream, the man who woke me only once to ask for comfort, the man who walked down the street in his too short pants, the pants that were never too short when he was well and loved to do his own wash, always on delicate, dried outdoors on the line by the star dogwood, the man who kept the winds from blowing too hard on me, the man who said, *Even death can be a healing*.

## NOW THAT YOU ARE SPIRIT

I am trying to learn what is contained in silence—
shining black ship against clear black sky—on nights
I am spacious as sea, my channel clears to let complicated

or splendid or refugee ships sail through—hulls fill with ghosts—
not the father or the desolate ancestors, but
spirits that belong to no one or to anyone in need.

Here fall comes to land and the colors of death are not silent—
golden-red leaves in reckless chorus, droves of dark birds
in the trees, beating of breasts on the Day of Atonement,

whoosh of your spirit departing from your body, rip of black
ribbon I will wear for seven days—because black contains
all colors, silence contains all this tearing apart.

What will I do now darling, with the honey in my loins,
my desire to know again the pleasures of your feather touch on
my skin trickling onto my thighs like rains and

brooks and ecstatic light even though in the end you
lay on your side with only the strength to breathe
onto my shoulder and that became enough.

And what will I do without the long and short sounds of
your heart that hummed through my chest and turned into
ribbons of bright color that rolled over my banks

of ribs, swelled like the River Rha after strong rains, and
spilled out onto reeds, into marshes, and into the mouths of
gulls? What will I do with all this Splendor you left me?

*Live!* You implored while your voice was just a whisper.
Now that you are spirit I hear you singing:
*My spirit sails through you like wind.*

*I can sail through anything.*
*I know where I am going.*
*I know how to steer myself home.*

*In living and in dying, be your own kind of ship—*
*signaling, shining, signaling. And when it is your turn,*
*do not ask how you will find me. I will find you.*

## BE KIND

Be kind to me and linger,
be in two places at once,
with your new life eternal
and with me in the woods

climbing toward the statue
of the Indian who looks
out onto the land that once
was his, that once was ours.

A light snow falls
without you,
I do not remember
myself without you.

Lunar crevasses
in my cheeks,
our child grown and graying,
you, a vertical pink cloud,

lavender arms of dusk
the day before snow,
face of the moon
during daylight.

## INK BLOTS

When you show long time meditators a Rorschach inkblot they see only splats of black on white, lines and curves, fat dots and tiny ones, instead of seeing butterflies, bulls, horses or blackbirds. They do not turn a vertical splash of ink into a waterfall of flowing hair of the dead beloved. They see only the way the ink has dripped onto the paper, the way the white receives the blackness. They do not turn the sky into a blessing.

## WHAT I MEAN BY BEAUTY


What I mean by beauty is not the strange red sky
you said belonged only to me or the regular blue sky
with white clouds you claimed as your own, because
you believed, you said, only what you could see.

What I mean by beauty is how you trusted me,
let my words wash over you, though you had
no idea what I was talking about when I said,
*The sky's fire-red feet rake across our bodies.*

What I mean by beauty is not the brilliant broach
of white moon against the eloquent deep blue,
the kind of blue that enunciates and disrobes
in the parking lot at the Home Depot.

I mean how the heavyset couple walks out
of the store side by side, how each then drifts,
one in front of the other, how they look happy,
unadorned, with white PVC piping poking out

of the super-sized orange cart, how they indulge
me when I point to the sliver of moon the way
a child might. How the woman with a blond-streaked
wig stops her jalopy beside me, her front seat filled

with marked-down shiny fat-leafed rubber plants,
how she says, *I see you got some too!* Though
I got coreopsis with spidery leaves, pale yellow flowers,
tiny stars, I agree with her since she just wants to say

from One came many and how we need each other.
What I mean by beauty is when I point to the moon,
the woman with the bright abundant wig laughs and says,
*Ya gotta love that!* How she doesn't turn her head

to look back at the white crescent. She is sure of love
as she drives off with her rubber plants. What I mean
by beauty is freedom; when I say freedom I mean how
the moon lifts us, scats us into the deep curve of her hip.

# SPECIAL THANKS

With deep gratitude to: Leslie Ullman, for her careful and thoughtful editing; M. Scott Douglass for believing in my work and publishing this book; Susan Deikman for patient, creative, collaborative front cover design; my son, Ari Halbert, for creative and deeply thoughtful type face treatment in front cover design; Kathleen Eastwood for providing the mysterious, beautiful cover art painting; M. Scott Douglass for back cover design and integrating the cover as a whole; Mary Richardson Miller, Hayden Saunier, and Janice Wilson Stridick, for four years of nurturing and helpful biweekly critique group; Chris Bursk for encouragement and critique of an early draft of the manuscript; Grant Clauser, founder of the Wordshop and members: Neil Babcox, Fran Baird, Liz Chang, Susan Charkes, Joanne Leva, Helen Mirkil, Hayden Saunier, and Amy Small-McKinney, for support and critique of individual poems in the book; Randall Couch for support and edits of several poems in the manuscript; Joanne Leva for founding and nourishing the Montgomery County Poet Laureate Program; Bread Loaf Writers Conference and Vermont College of Fine Arts for manuscript workshops under the tutelage of Louise Gluck, Major Jackson, and Kevin Young; Chris Bursk and the Bucks County Poetry Community for ongoing support; Polly Young-Eisendrath for continued encouragement and sustenance; Carol Hinzman for blessed friendship, deep listening and dance; my brother, David Ferleger, for emails of effusive praise as well as clarifying questions and suggestions; my beloved Steven Carl Halbert, whose love and devotion are forever cherished, who, on his deathbed, asked me to read to him many of the poems contained in this book, and who then wept with joy as he said, *my wife is a poet.*